Moon Over Snow's

Greg Artkop

Moon Over Snow's

© 2024 Greg Artkop

Adriel Publishing

ALL RIGHTS RESERVED. No part of this book may be reproduced in any form or by any means whatsoever, including photography, xerography, broadcast, transmission, translation into any language, or recording, without permission in writing from the publisher. Reviewers may quote brief passages in critical articles or reviews.

Printed in the U.S.A.

Cover Design and Illustrations by Hatice Bayramoglu

ISBN: 979-8-9893049-4-3

www.SNOWSBBQ.com

Dedication

First and most important, to God, all the glory to Him!

To the ENTIRE staff of Snow's BBQ, who have always gone above and beyond.

To our awesome customers, who continue to show up each Saturday, order online, and eat our BBQ. Y'all are the real MVPs.

To our BBQ family, we would not want to do this with anyone else.

To Ms. Tootsie, the Queen of BBQ, who is an inspiration to all.

Kerry & Kim Bexley

It's midnight in Texas,

the moon shines down

On a shack in the center of

Lexington town

The silos are glowing,

the smoke's in the air

The cars start arriving from

everywhere

It's quiet as a cow starts to

moo in the shed

And the fire gently pops in

its round iron bed

As the line starts to build and

the chairs begin snapping

And the snores begin snoring

as the people start napping

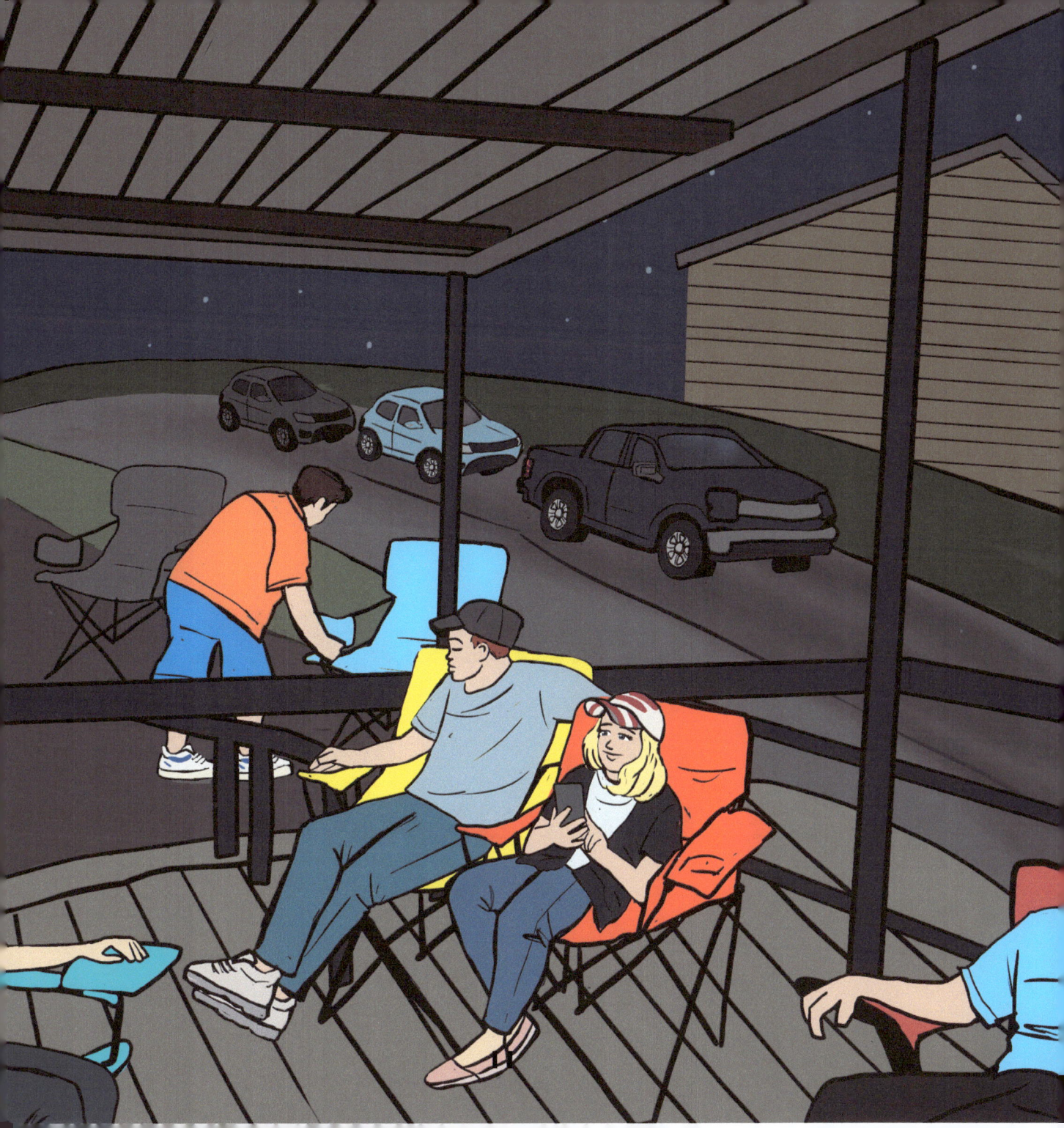

The air wet with dew mixed

with smokey delight

As the pitmasters work in

the dim moonlit night

While the flames dance and glow

Burning bright from the wood,

dry post oak will always

make everything good

And then, all at once,

around 6 in the morning

they're talking, and walking

as the news begins dawning

17

"Miss Tootsie is here,"

they jump up for a view

And a pic with the famous

Queen of BBQ

She stokes the fire slowly,

shovels coals red and hot

And she's mopping the meat,

tasty drop after drop

It's brisket for breakfast,

sausage, turkey and ribs

Pork steaks so juicy you just

might need two bibs

Salt, pepper, wood, fire,

smoke and meat

Are the magical recipe for

the best Texas treat

WELCOME TO SNOW'S

MENU

BRISKET, PORK, RIBS, CHICKEN, PORK STEAK, Reg & Jal SAUSAGE

HOMEMADE...

POTATO SALAD, COLESLAW, BEANS

THANKS SO MUCH FOR YOUR BUSINESS!

We give thanks to the Lord,

in the morning we pray

For the moon over Snow's,

for the bright shining day

For the great state of Texas,

for the meal on your tray

Thank you kindly, from

Kerry, Miss Tootsie and Clay

Greg Artkop

It's fair to say that Greg Artkop (aka Buzztex) has a passion for BBQ. He visited the top 50 BBQ joints in Texas twice in four years. You might find him snoozing on the porch at Snow's or gazing at the Lexington moon, planning his next great BBQ trip. Greg's other children's book can be found at www.BabysFirstBBQ.com.

www.ingramcontent.com/pod-product-compliance
Lightning Source LLC
Chambersburg PA
CBHW051514110526
44582CB00007B/120